THE BALD EAGLE

by Cari Meister

PEBBLE
a capstone imprint

Published by Pebble, an imprint of Capstone
1710 Roe Crest Drive, North Mankato, Minnesota 56003
capstonepub.com

Library of Congress Cataloging-in-Publication Data is available on the Library of Congress website.

ISBN: 9798875248139 (hardcover)
ISBN: 9798875248085 (paperback)
ISBN: 9798875248092 (ebook PDF)

Summary: Simple text introduces readers to the bald eagle, explaining its history, meaning, and why it is an important symbol today.

Editorial Credits
Editor: Mandy Robbins; Designer: Sarah Bennett; Media Researcher: Rebekah Hubstenberger; Production Specialist: Tori Abraham

Image Credits
Alamy: Marilyn Angel Wynn, 13; Getty Images: aaaaimages, 20, Brendan Smialowski-Pool, 19, iStock/Brian Shoemaker, 15, iStock/Kandfoto, 21, iStock/pchoui, 5, Jamie Sabau, 7, Mark Newman, 9, Mark Newman, 16, Michael J. Cohen, Photographer, 8; Shutterstock: ANNA DOMINIKA (watercolor background), back cover and throughout, Borka Kiss, 11, Daniel Sobolic, 6, FloridaStock, front cover, SherryArts, 18

Printed and bound in China. 006460

Table of Contents

Words in **bold** are in the glossary

Our National Bird

Look up! Have you ever seen a bald eagle? It can **soar** high in the sky. The bald eagle is America's national bird. It is big and strong. It has a white head that looks like it's wearing a bright cap.

A bald eagle can see well. It can spot **prey** from far away. It can see a tiny fish from the top of a tall tree.

A bald eagle has a huge **wingspan**. Its wings can spread 7.5 feet (2.3 meters) wide. That's taller than most grown-ups.

Bald eagles **mate** for life. The pair builds a nest together. The female lays one to three eggs.

Eagles can live for 30 years. That's longer than most dogs and cats!

The Story of Our Eagle

In 1782, the United States was a new country. It needed a Presidential **Seal**. Leaders wanted a bird on it, but they couldn't agree on which one. Then Charles Thomson chose the bald eagle. Other leaders approved.

SEAL OF THE PRESIDENT OF THE UNITED STATES
E PLURIBUS UNUM

The bald eagle was only found in North America. It could fly higher than any other bird. It was brave and free. Native peoples in the United States had honored eagles for ages. Some tribes use eagle feathers in special **ceremonies**.

What the Bald Eagle Stands For

The bald eagle stands for strength. It is a powerful bird! It grabs fish from lakes and rivers. Its claws hold on as it flies away. An eagle soars through the sky without flapping its wings much. It rides the wind, free as can be. It reminds us of freedom.

Bald eagles build nests high up in tall trees. They watch over the land. They remind us to guard our land and freedom. Bald eagles teach their young to be strong and **independent**.

Our Eagle Today

Today, you can spot bald eagle **symbols** in many places. It is still on the President's Seal. It is on the backs of some quarters and dollar bills. It is on important buildings. But the most exciting way to see an eagle is in nature!

E PLURIBUS UNUM

Eagles remind us to take care of nature. Bald eagles almost disappeared from America. Farmers used sprays that hurt eagle eggs. Leaders passed laws against using the spray. Now there are many more eagles!

Draw Your Own Eagle!

Draw and color your own bald eagle. Use colored paper. Give it a white head and yellow beak and claws.

What do you want it to do? Is it flying in the sky? Is it sitting in its nest? Is it catching a big fish?

Glossary

ceremony (SAYR-uh-moh-nee)—actions, words, or music performed to mark an important event

independent (in-di-PEN-duhnt)—free from the control of other people or things

mate (MAYT)—to join together to produce young

prey (PRAY)—an animal hunted as food

seal (SEEL)—a design pressed into an important paper or envelope

soar (SOR)—to fly without flapping wings much

symbol (SIM-buhl)—a design or an object that stands for something else

wingspan (WING-span)—how wide a bird's wings are when spread out

Can You Remember?

1. Why did American leaders choose the bald eagle as a symbol?

2. What color is a bald eagle's head?

3. What helped save the bald eagles from disappearing?

Index

About the Author

Cari Meister lives in Vail, Colorado, with her family and rescue dog. Cari is a children's librarian and the author of more than 300 books. She enjoys reading, skiing, yoga, running, and riding her horse, Sir William.